Praise

"I really loved this book. Its presentation is so simple and it dre........ .... reading the many alphatudes and realized how valuable they can be to one's daily life, helping anyone keep focused on truth and life itself. It's a must on everyone's bookshelf."
—**James Twyman**, best-selling author of *The Moses Code*

"*Alphatudes: The Alphabet of Gratitude* demonstrates just how easy it really is to count your blessings. This book provides a fun and practical method for increasing your awareness of the many opportunities for gratitude that exist in your life right now."
—**Mike Robbins**, author of *Focus on the Good Stuff*

"Michele Wahlder has created a practical and delightful method for opening the heart to the joy and benefits of gratitude. Whether in the simplest experiences of everyday life or in the most elevated spiritual encounters, it is up to us to choose to find the good, and then to turn our hearts to that gift in gratitude. *Alphatudes* shows us how to accomplish that in a systematic way that solidly roots the attitude of gratitude in the depths of consciousness and soul. This book is a gift to all who would lift and open their hearts to the blessings concealed within."
—**Alan Morinis**, author of *Everyday Holiness* & founder of The Mussar Institute

"This book will make you feel better! You will love *Alphatudes* from the moment it enters your life. Opening it will fill you with gratitude to be holding such a beautiful, inspiring book, filled with encouraging words and images."
—**Jana Stanfield**, recording artist

"Michele Wahlder presents a simple tool in which a powerful meditation on gratitude can be structured using the ABCs. The delectably transporting illustrations, along with the well-worded affirmations and prayers that accompany each of the twenty-six entries, support the book's luminous bouquet. It is recommended without reservation!"
—**Mount Shasta Magazine**

"In *Alphatudes*, Michele Wahlder gives us a rich palette of truths. Each of her twenty-six reflections, matched with vibrant illustrations, allows us to transform ingrained neural patterns so that gratitude becomes our natural response to life's gifts."
—**Brother David Steindl-Rast**, author of *Gratefulness, the Heart of Prayer* & co-founder of Gratefulness.org

alphatudes

the alphabet of gratitude

alphatudes

the alphabet of gratitude

MICHELE WAHLDER

LifePossibilities
PUBLISHING

Life Possibilities Publishing
An Imprint of Life Possibilities, LLC
5930 Royal Lane, #296
Dallas, TX 75230
lifepossibilities.com

The text in this book is set in Nueva STD

Manufactured in Malaysia

ISBN 10: 0-9823645-0-4
ISBN 13: 978-0-9823645-0-5

Dedication

To the colorfully elegant, gently loving and vibrantly enchanting memory of my mother, Nurit Pilzer Wahlder. And to the strong, supportive and unconditionally loving memory of my grandmothers, Yohanna "Hansi" Altman Pilzer and Bernice Mansberg Wahlder.

alphatude | *noun*

a person, place or thing for which one
alphabetically expresses gratitude

alphatudes

Contents

Preface

Many years ago, I was having a bout of sleeplessness that lasted weeks. Exhausted and at my wit's end, I was struck with an idea: *Instead of counting sheep, what if I counted my blessings?* I needed a simple yet methodical way to lull my mind and ease my spirit into a place of restfulness. I started with the letter A and thought of apples. I consciously focused on how grateful I was to have such a wide variety of apples to enjoy. I thought of their many robust colors and flavors: red, golden, green, Fuji, Pink Lady, Granny Smith. My mind then moved on to the letter B as I imagined the beauty of the sunset I was blessed to witness earlier in the evening. A pattern of gratitude had begun! I proceeded to the letter C; I selected "coat" and thought about how grateful I was for the comfy, cozy coat that had kept me warm all winter long. D was easy—my dog. He is a constant reminder that no matter how busy I am, there is always time to play. I continued my reflection upon the alphabet of gratitude and was soon catching ZZZs.

I woke up the next day feeling energized and rejuvenated. I soon began to build on this newfound gift of gratitude as a way of clearing my mind and processing the events of the day in a positive way. Eagerly sharing my method with clients and friends, I began receiving feedback that the ABCs of gratitude were changing lives for the better, and so *Alphatudes: The Alphabet of Gratitude* was born.

Over time, I experienced a profound shift in my life as my awareness of the numerous opportunities for gratitude grew each day. While I still encounter the typical challenges inherent in the ebb and flow of life, my perspective is now ultimately to find the blessing rather than to focus on the problem. As I integrated alphatudes into my life and coaching practice, my desire grew to share this concept with a wider audience. I am certain you will discover, as I have, that the more you share the miracle of gratitude, the more it comes back to you.

Acknowledgments

God, thank you for gifting my soul with this book. I believe that you were gently molding and preparing me to communicate these inspirational teachings long before I was consciously aware of them. Only through your divine encouragement, guidance and support have I been able to bring the concept of "alphatudes" into being.

I am forever grateful to my spiritual mentor, Nina LaSalle. You have provided me with the best example of a "grateful person" I could have ever hoped for. You continually inspire me to be my best version of myself. I would not be the woman I am today without your faithful guidance and loving support.

Through your inspiring light and encouraging friendship, you have empowered me to reach my dreams. Thank you, Ann Brooks.

Leasta Roberts, Rosa Smith and Lillian Cotton, your unconditional love and kindness continue to comfort and nourish me.

Cindy Nixon of Bookmarker Editorial Services, you are a joy to work with and an editor extraordinaire!

Bethany Brown, Amy Collins MacGregor (of the Cadence Group) and Gwyn Kennedy Snider (of GKS Creative), thank you for the professionalism, integrity and invaluable experience you provided in bringing *Alphatudes* to the marketplace in its best possible form.

Tom Beckman, thank you for reminding me that writing is rewriting.

I am deeply grateful to my friend John McGill for practicing my alphabet of gratitude process, thereby providing me with the motivation to move forward with my project.

Michael Wahlder, through your powerful example, you continuously inspire me to enthusiastically go for what I desire in life. Thank you, Dad.

Michael Kerber, you are the love of my life and my most faithful supporter. Your optimistic outlook, unwavering encouragement and calm strength carried me through the writing of this book. I feel incredibly grateful to share my life with you.

I am immensely grateful to the friends, clients, colleagues and teachers who contributed directly and indirectly to this book.

*Grow flowers of gratitude in the
soil of prayer.*

Verbena Woods

Introduction

Alphatudes: The Alphabet of Gratitude utilizes the ABCs as an easy and methodical structure for developing a sustainable consciousness of gratitude. What simpler way to positively transform our outlook on life than through a system we conquered as children? An "alphatude" is defined as a person, place or thing for which one alphabetically expresses gratitude. You will be guided on a beautifully inspiring journey through twenty-six alphatudes drawn from spiritual principles and universal human concepts. The alphatudes offered in this book are enhanced with inspirational quotes, breathtaking illustrations, insightful teachings, affirmative statements and heartfelt prayers. You will not only grow in your practice of gratitude, you will connect with the God of your understanding and discover the serenity and prosperity that is already yours.

Becoming truly appreciative of our lives requires us to replace our negative, limiting thoughts with positive, affirming words that strengthen our feeling of optimism. Language is one of the primary ways we perceive and understand our world and one of the key tools we rely on to connect to others. Each word we use has an emotional charge that either nurtures our well-being or creates a sense of discord within our essence. *Alphatudes: The Alphabet of Gratitude* helps us become aware of how our vocabulary forms the language through which we experience our lives. When we consciously choose to use words of gratitude to describe our human journey and the world we live in, we assume responsibility for our own happiness.

We often exert our energy—physically, emotionally and intellectually—to obtain more of what we think we want and need to make us happy. Our society bombards us with messages that reinforce the notion that we are deficient in some way and desperately need to upgrade ourselves and our lifestyles. Eventually, many of us succumb to the seductive "new and improved" marketing strategies that are so pervasive in our culture, resulting in the mistaken belief that if we could only have a particular thing, circumstance or relationship, we would then be happy and fulfilled. This belief that our happiness is contingent upon something outside of ourselves keeps us in a perpetual state of dissatisfaction. By relying on the equation *If only _____, then I would be happy*, we actually strengthen the inaccurate perception that we are not enough: *If only I lost weight, had fewer wrinkles, made more money, had more confidence … then I would be happy*. We keep postponing our happiness, waiting for "one day" when we will have achieved all that we falsely believe makes us worthy of fully enjoying our lives. The problem is that "one day" rarely comes; and if it does, the pleasure derived from our accomplishment is usually fleeting as we quickly set our sights on our next "happiness goal."

Through the conscious practice of gratitude, we are able to find within ourselves a deep well of joyful appreciation for what we already have. The Hebrew term for the word "gratitude" is *hakarat ha'tov,* literally translated as "recognizing the good." When we recognize and focus on the good in our lives, we are making the choice to embrace the sweetness of life and live fully aware of our divine abundance. When we take time to be grateful for our daily bounty, we begin to feel a warm, enveloping sense of appreciation. This is the essence of gratitude.

We cultivate gratitude when we trust in a divine plan and humbly understand that with our limited vision, we cannot possibly see the whole picture or completely grasp all of the reasons why our lives, and the lives of those we love, have unfolded as they have. Everything is a gift, whether we can appreciate it at the time or not. Often at a later date, with thoughtful reflection, we are blessed with a precious glimpse of insight and clarity.

Alphatudes: The Alphabet of Gratitude brings to our awareness many everyday concepts that are a part of our human experience. When we choose to be grateful for these concepts, we evolve into more illuminated spiritual beings, making our human adventure here on this earth more joyful and fulfilling. As we increasingly become aware of and grateful for our blessings, the appreciation that resides within us grows, deepens and radiates brightly into our world.

The Action of Gratitude

In his book *Thanks! How Practicing Gratitude Can Make You Happier,* world-renowned scientist, author and leader in the field of gratitude Robert A. Emmons, Ph.D., defines gratitude as "a deep and abiding recognition and acknowledgment that goodness exists under even the worst that life offers." Within my profession, I witness time and again that it is indeed during life's most challenging moments that we find our greatest opportunity for evolving into the highest vision we hold for ourselves. These challenging life moments are moments of choice—a metaphorical fork in the road. How we choose to deal with these pivotal times in our lives determines how we grow as human and spiritual beings. Gratitude, as both an action and a state of consciousness, is the foundation that moves us into our greatest life possibilities and our best version of ourselves. By choosing to be grateful and acknowledging the good, even in the toughest situations, we accept the divine challenge to expand beyond our current emotional, psychological and spiritual state of being.

To utilize the concept of gratitude as a channel for evolving into our highest vision of ourselves, we must take action. Conceptually, gratitude is a positive shift in our perception of any given situation or circumstance, but the action of gratitude takes the concept into a transformative state.

In his book *Evolve Your Brain: The Science of Changing Your Mind*, Dr. Joe Dispenza explains that our brains are comprised of neural networks or pathways. Just as a well-worn path becomes increasingly worn through constant traffic or activity, so do our neural networks become increasingly entrenched through continuous firing. With each thought and/or action we take, a specific neurological pathway fires off a connection that becomes more deeply ingrained in our brains and therefore our behavior and thought patterns. Likewise, as a pathway or trail ceases to have traffic, vines, grass and other matter grow over the trail until it eventually disappears completely.

As we change our thought patterns, new networks develop and the old networks begin to die off. We can literally change our genetic makeup through conscious and deliberate control of our thoughts. The words "conscious" and "deliberate" are key to this process. Just as we drive a car without consciously thinking about the next step—unlock the door, sit down, shut the door, put the key in the ignition and so on—we elicit certain behaviors and thought patterns with such deep neural networks that we are on autopilot when performing these actions. Neural networks that function on autopilot are functioning in the subconscious—actions and thoughts of which we are not consciously aware.

Our subconscious belief systems impact all aspects of our being, from relationships and career to finances to our physical and mental well-being. We do not have to be held hostage by these deeply ingrained neural networks, some of which we may have been born with. Through the conscious and deliberate practice of gratitude, we can quite literally transform our brains and change our lives for the better.

Choosing Gratitude

Gratitude is a choice. It may or may not be a particular person's natural state of being, but it is an option available to all. We can choose to be grateful in specific circumstances as well as to live in a continuous and deliberate state of gratitude. In *Thanks!* Emmons writes, "gratitude is morally and intellectually demanding." Emmons goes on to explain that by choosing to be grateful, "we sharpen our ability to recognize and acknowledge the giftedness of life. It means that we make a conscious choice to see blessings instead of curses. It means that our internal reactions are not determined by external forces." As we choose to practice gratitude over a period of time, we are able to significantly increase our personal range of happiness.

When we choose gratitude in a challenging circumstance, we are making the internal choice to see the good and trust that the circumstance, no matter how difficult, will provide an opportunity for divine illumination.

Each day we are all presented with situations that are beyond our control, but in each situation we are in complete control of our perception and response to the situation. For example, many times we are involved in unexpected traffic, causing us to be late to an important event. We can use this time in anger, frustration or even panic, sending our cortisol levels soaring and increasing toxic chemicals in our bodies, or we can choose to be grateful for the additional time to sit in the quiet of our car and mentally prepare for the event, pray or even catch up on phone calls. The traffic is beyond our control; how we respond to the traffic is completely within our control.

> *"As we choose to practice gratitude over a period of time, we are able to significantly increase our personal range of happiness."*

Our bodies elicit a chemical reaction to every emotion we experience. In her book *You Can Heal Your Life*, Louise Hay discusses the physical response our bodies have to a multitude of both negative and positive thoughts. The good news is that we can change our lives by changing our thoughts. Just as a change in diet creates a change in our physical bodies, so does changing our thought patterns change our brain and thereby the way we perceive and experience life.

Practicing Gratitude

If we decide to lose weight, we must change our eating habits for longer than one day. If we want to save money, we must curb our spending for more than one day. If we want to make a high score on a test, we must study more than one time. So it is with the practice of gratitude. If we want to change the neural networks in our brain to be our best version of ourselves, we must be consistent. The practice of gratitude is always a journey rather than a destination.

Frequency in our practice of gratitude is directly related to the paradigm shift we experience. The more we express gratitude, the more positively we perceive the world and our experiences in the world. Consequently, the more frequently we perceive positive experiences, the more frequently the positive experiences occur. One principle of quantum physics states that we will experience or find that which we expect to experience or find. In other words, our expectations are self-fulfilling. Therefore, the more we expect to experience opportunities for gratitude, the more opportunities we will be presented.

In her book *The How of Happiness: A New Approach to Getting the Life You Want*, Sonja Lyubomirsky, Ph.D., explains the determining factors for an individual's level of happiness. Lyubomirsky discovered that 50 percent of the recipe for happiness is actually a genetically determined natural set point—10 percent is determined by a person's circumstances and 40 percent is determined by intentional activity. If 50 percent of our perceived level of happiness is genetically predisposed, science suggests that we are not "condemned" to a fate determined by our genes. While we may or may not be able to influence the 10 percent of our life circumstances, we can certainly choose how we respond to life. With 40 percent of our perceived happiness being determined by intentional activity, we have more than ample room for elevating our level of happiness. Lyubomirsky suggests that a conscious practice of expressing our gratitude is one of the best ways to increase happiness in our lives. Research confirms that there are numerous physical, emotional, spiritual and mental benefits to practicing gratitude.

"The practice of gratitude is always a journey rather than a destination."

How to Use This Book

Familiarize yourself with the alphatudes presented in this book by first reading through it once. Allow the alphabet of gratitude to nourish you as you focus on the spiritual principles of gratitude, prayer and affirmative statements offered. You can then, on a daily or weekly basis, go back through the book and intuitively choose an alphatude that speaks to your heart. You may find that sitting quietly with a concept you would like to explore more deeply helps you further your personal awareness of the alphatude and assists you in moving forward on your spiritual path. During times of contemplation and reflection, you can feed your soul, revitalize your spirit and get clear about your life.

Each of the twenty-six alphatudes opens with a quote that expresses the essence of that particular alphatude. Creatively paired with each quote is an illustration to visually assist you in absorbing the teaching. Allow the colorfully enchanting images and corresponding quotes to transport you into a receptive state of consciousness, preparing you in the process to more fully assimilate the meaning of the concepts.

The illustrations, quotes and narratives are accompanied by life-affirming statements that will strengthen your overall sense of well-being. When stated from a place of genuine belief and sincere gratitude for their universal truths, these powerful statements can profoundly influence the quality of your life. Reading and/or speaking these statements is a method for shifting into a grateful and positive mind-set. Over time, by replacing negative thoughts with positive beliefs, you can penetrate your subconscious mind, elevate your consciousness and create personally beneficial changes.

Following each of the affirmative statements is a prayer. Use these prayers to invite the God of your understanding into your life to support you on your journey of appreciation. When we pray, we actively let go and ask God to assist and guide us in accessing solutions and possibilities we may never have come to by ourselves. Prayer is the process of raising our thoughts above the human plane and connecting to a realm of spiritual resourcefulness that does not depend on us alone. Through prayer, we surrender our self-will, reach out in faith and fill ourselves with hope. In prayer, we acknowledge our trust in the presence of God and bolster our faith in the belief that things will work out, even if we don't know exactly how. We can relieve ourselves of the heavy burdens we have tried to carry on our own and are willing to watch life unfold the way God would have it be. During prayer and meditation, we can transcend much of the darkness in our lives and choose to stand grounded in the light of God. As we pray, we increase our capacity to embrace the mystery of life. We admit that we do not have all the answers and that miracles can and do happen. When we let go of our need to control, we can feel the peace that comes from being connected to and relying on God.

I coined the term "alphatudes" as a way to incorporate a vocabulary of gratitude into our language. By utilizing this fun and practical tool for methodically increasing gratitude in our lives, we positively transform our personal and collective consciousness. Use this book as a foundation for creating your own personal alphatudes and for continuously expanding your vocabulary of gratitude. Journaling your daily blessings is another meaningful way to deepen your gratitude practice through the written word. You may also want to work through this book with a friend, a group, a spiritual adviser or a life coach to help you integrate and apply the concepts in your life.

My hope for you is that as you grow in gratitude, it will become a natural reaction to the events in your life and will allow you to build a more positive relationship with yourself and the world around you.

May you find peace and joy through gratitude.
With love, light and thankfulness,

Michele Wahlder

Acceptance

I saw a star, I reached for it, I missed,
so I accepted the sky.

Scott Fortini

Acceptance

I am grateful for Acceptance.

Acceptance is a peace-filled acknowledgment that everything is exactly as it should be in the present moment. Only through acceptance are we able to create the bridge that leads to our highest visions of ourselves. The spiritual teacher and author Iyanla Vanzant said, "God loves you and accepts you because you are a part of God." As we learn to love and accept ourselves exactly as we are in each moment, we move into the greatness that divinely resides in each and every one of us. Acceptance allows us to see ourselves as God sees us.

When we lovingly accept our virtues as well as our shortcomings, we become less judgmental and more compassionate. Our relationships transform because we are no longer trying to control and manipulate the people in our lives to be who we think they should be. Instead, we are able to take constructive action based on the truth of "what is" today, whether we like it or not. As we release the fantasy of wishing that people or circumstances were different, we gain the energy necessary to enjoy life and passionately pursue our own goals and dreams.

Acceptance does not mean that we choose to remain in unhappy or unhealthy circumstances or that we refuse to grow and improve. However, it does mean that we choose to accept and love ourselves as we are and the world exactly as it is, right now, regardless of the future changes we hope to make. We are, in essence, gratefully admitting that through our willpower alone, we cannot change ourselves, the world or other people for the purpose of meeting our own expectations. Through acceptance, we are able to cultivate the inner peace and resolve necessary to build a new and healthier reality for ourselves.

I am willing to release the pain between how things are and how I think they should be. I choose to be peaceful and content with "what is" today. I love and accept myself just as I am, right now.

Prayer of Acceptance

Infuse me with the faith to surrender to you those things that
are outside of my control. Provide me with the wisdom and
strength to change what I can. Thank you for blessing me with
the freedom and serenity that comes from acceptance.

Beauty

*Beauty is not in the face,
beauty is a light in the heart.*

Kahlil Gibran

Beauty
I am grateful for Beauty.

Beauty is revealed from the inside out. We only need look within our own hearts to find the beauty we are so desperately seeking. In our current culture, we are bombarded with advertising and messages telling us that "we are not enough" as we are and that "we do not have enough" material possessions to be acceptable. When we get caught up in this competitive cycle of comparing ourselves to others, we lose. However, when we appreciate and admire ourselves just as we are, we win. Beauty is present in each moment and can only be experienced when we cease trying to make it better, different or more than it already is.

Ralph Waldo Emerson, American transcendentalist, said, "Though we travel the world over to find the beautiful, we must carry it with us or we find it not." When we make the conscious choice to slow down, we begin to notice the beauty that exists all around us. As we focus our attention on the glorious splendor that is right in front of our eyes, we experience a positive inner shift that awakens and delights our senses. As we pause to enjoy the simple things in life, we become aware of the beauty that is, and always was, right here.

Take time to explore your world in a different way today. Soak in all the beauty that surrounds you. Gaze into the eyes of those you love and acknowledge the beauty of their heart. Honor the magic in your routine by pouring your morning beverage into a special cup. Observe the dancing shadows and light patterns in your home. Treat yourself to the gift of fragrant flowers. Look at yourself in the mirror and appreciate your unique loveliness. Allow yourself to absorb the magnificence and wonder of nature's divine creations. Appreciate the extraordinary beauty that exists in the ordinary.

I see the beauty in everyone and everything, including myself.
I feel my beauty radiating out from my heart into all of my
relationships and into the world. I am beautiful.

Prayer of Beauty

Help me to experience the timeless beauty within my heart and soul. Open my eyes to all the beautiful gifts you have bestowed upon me and the earth. Thank you for allowing me to be a part of your beautiful creation.

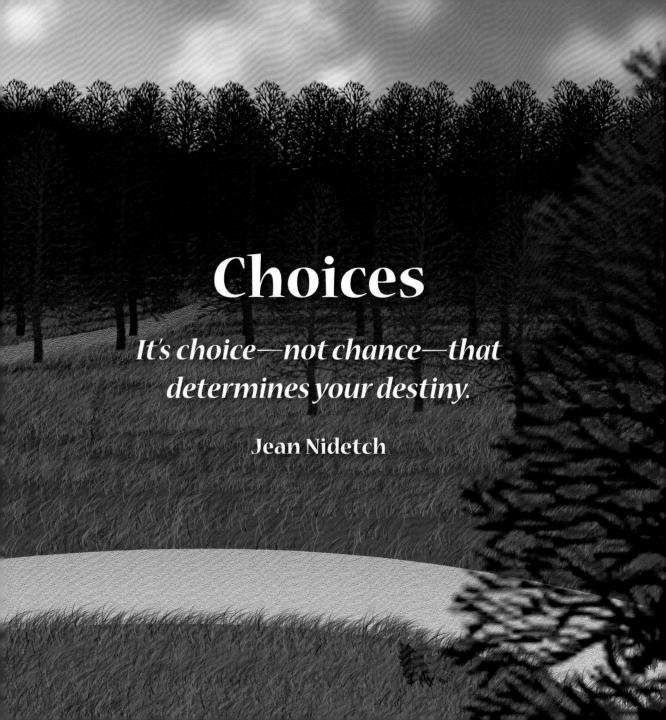

Choices

It's choice—not chance—that determines your destiny.

Jean Nidetch

Choices

I am grateful for Choices.

Choices offer us hope and unlimited possibilities. Our lives are really the sum of our choices; when we change our choices, we change our lives. Each choice we make today will impact the direction of our future. The Austrian neurologist, psychiatrist and Holocaust survivor Viktor E. Frankl said, "To choose one's attitude in any given set of circumstances is to choose one's own way." Many times, we may feel as though we have no choices; however, we always have the power to choose our attitude, our actions and our responses.

When we engage in unconscious decision-making out of habit or fear, we tend to repeat our past patterns, which predictably produce the same old results. If we want to reach our goals and life dreams, we must mindfully explore all of our options and make fresh, new choices that align with the life we truly desire. We must give up the need for the approval of others in order to make authentic choices that result in more self-confidence, inner peace and fulfillment. The quality of our choices truly reflects the amount of love we have for ourselves.

Often we need to gather additional information to make an intelligent choice about how to proceed. While this is a valuable part of the decision-making process, it is vital to remember that our answers are already inside of us in each moment. Taking the time to get quiet, breathe deeply and check in with our own inner truth can help us make decisions that are in our best interest. Choices that are in alignment with our souls' desires increase our energy, while choices that are not in our highest good drain our energy. In order to make positive, life-enhancing choices, it is crucial to get in touch with the divine information and guidance that resides within.

I courageously make choices that propel me forward into the life I desire. I easily release the need for other people's approval. I choose options that are in alignment with my inner truth.

Prayer of Choices

Help me to clearly see all the choices and options available to me. Give me the clarity I need to make choices that are in my highest good. Thank you for inspiring me to choose that which will bring me closer to your will for me.

Dreams

*Only as high as I reach can I grow,
only as far as I seek can I go, only as
deep as I look can I see, only as
much as I dream can I be.*

Karen Ravn

I am grateful for Dreams.

Dreams provide a window into the world of our infinite potential. Some people believe our souls travel to other times and places when we dream, providing us with experiences and understandings we could never actually have in our physical bodies. Whether our soul literally or figuratively travels is inconsequential because the end result is the same—a deeper understanding and a broader perspective of ourselves. Through this expanded view, we can then dare to dream of a new reality for our waking life.

Both sleeping and waking dreams provide the seeds that sprout into our lives' possibilities. Oftentimes, we sow our dream seeds unconsciously. When we allow our thoughts to wander into the realms of what "could have been" or "should have been," we sow seeds of discontent. But when we dare to dream of "what could be" and "what is possible," we plant seeds that grow with joyful expectancy, purpose and intention.

Our dreams have a ripple effect that impacts those around us. Sometimes this ripple effect is small, but sometimes our dreams can create change in the lives of thousands and even millions of people. Martin Luther King Jr. demonstrated how immensely powerful our dreams are when we have the courage to follow them. Our dreams can continue to impact humanity long after we leave this lifetime. When we dream consciously and fearlessly, the potential for positive impact can expand far beyond our wildest imaginings.

I am open and receptive to the messages I receive in my dreams.
I passionately and boldly follow my dreams. I dare to dream big.

Prayer of Dreams

Help me to unravel the mystery of my dreams. Guide me in using my dreams to deepen my self-awareness and create a more positive world. Thank you for the sense of hope that dreams inspire in all of us.

Emotions

Sadness flowers to the next renewing joy.

Jareb Teague

Emotions

I am grateful for Emotions.

Emotions serve as messengers that communicate with us and simply ask to be heard and acknowledged. While there are emotions that feel better to experience than others, there are no good or bad emotions. When we lovingly honor and tend to our internal emotional landscape, we experience greater mental, physical, spiritual and relational health. However, when we dismiss the signals our emotions and instincts are alerting us to, we may experience dis-ease, which can manifest as various ailments in all levels of our being. John Gottman, Ph.D., world-renowned for his work in marital stability, writes, "Researchers have found that even more than IQ, your emotional awareness and ability to handle feelings will determine your success and happiness in all walks of life."

When we suppress emotions such as sadness, anger, fear or grief, we bury energy that is alive and desperately needs to be acknowledged, soothed and then released. When left unattended, this energy festers and irritates us in an attempt to get our attention. These emotions do not die; they remain lodged in our psyches and bodies until, ultimately, we are forced to confront, and thereby learn from, the emotional issues that cause us pain.

Accepting all of our emotions means we become respectful observers and responsible stewards of them. We need to embrace our emotions as part of us and know that regardless of how pleasant or unpleasant they may be, their intentions are good. As we sit with our emotions and thank them for their innate wisdom, we become receptive to the lessons they have to teach us. Once empathetically heard and honored, they can easily and peacefully dissolve, having served their purpose.

I embrace the rich tapestry of emotions that are part of my human experience. I lovingly welcome all of my emotions and value their presence in my life. I express my emotions honestly and respectfully.

Prayer of Emotions

Help me to peacefully coexist with all of my emotions.
Sustain me as I willingly accept and learn from the lessons my
emotions have to offer. Thank you for blessing me with a wide
range of emotional expression.

Forgiveness

Forgiveness is the fragrance that the violet sheds on the heel that has crushed it.

Mark Twain

Forgiveness

I am grateful for Forgiveness.

Forgiveness is a gift we give ourselves. Only through forgiveness are we able to liberate ourselves from the person or situation that caused us pain and truly begin to heal. Alexander Pope once stated, "To err is human, to forgive is divine." When we offer sincere, heartfelt forgiveness, we function from the divinity that resides in us all. When we carry a grudge and hold on to the mistaken belief that the person who hurt us does not deserve to be forgiven, we are operating from the human ego.

Sincere forgiveness is not necessarily about accepting or granting an apology; an apology may never be extended. However, through the act of forgiving, we learn to lovingly detach from the person who caused us pain, releasing ourselves from our own self-imposed prison. Forgiveness does not mean we have to accept or condone poor behavior; it simply means we choose to let go of the self-righteous stance that separates us from the light of God and our fellow human beings. Our question should not be, "Does this person deserve to be forgiven?" but rather, "Do I deserve the freedom and peace that comes from letting go of the hurt?" We do not have to forget, but we can release the negativity that binds us to past pain. We can consciously choose to free ourselves from the toxic resentment that causes us to suffer needlessly.

Oftentimes, the most challenging person to forgive is the one looking back at us in the mirror. We may have a tendency to be more critical of ourselves than we are of others. We may carry guilt or shame associated with the perception that we have disappointed someone we love. Before we can forgive another, we must first unconditionally forgive ourselves.

I am an embodiment of God's forgiving grace. I choose to release myself from the bondage of anger and resentment. I open my heart to the healing power of unconditional forgiveness.

Prayer of Forgiveness

Fill me with your divine capacity to love and forgive.
Cleanse every cell of my entire being of painful past
resentments. Thank you for the lightness
of spirit that comes from forgiveness.

Giving

*How far that little candle throws
its beams! So shines a good deed in
a naughty world.*

William Shakespeare

Giving
I am grateful for Giving.

Giving is its own reward. When we give to others, we share our divine inner light with them and help the world become a brighter, more illuminated place in which to live. Paradoxically, the act of giving to others begins with first giving to one's self. When we are physically, emotionally and spiritually satiated, we are able to joyfully give from a place of abundance. Initially, it may feel selfish to provide for ourselves—whether it is a nap, a half hour of quiet time or a walk in nature. However, giving to ourselves is essential if we are truly to be of service to others. We are each responsible for our own self-care so that we can have the capacity for generosity.

When we give to others, we give back to ourselves in return. The writer and philosopher Elbert Hubbard said, "Love grows by giving. The love we give away is the only love we keep." There is a natural flow of reciprocity inherent in giving. When we give with love in our hearts, we naturally receive delightful and unexpected gifts in return. Our own inner beauty and wisdom are magnified when we share hope, encouragement and love with another. However, when we give out of obligation, we tend to feel depleted and resentful. In order to experience the benefits of giving, it is important to be honest about the true intentions and motives behind our generosity.

Think back to a time in your life when someone's selfless act of giving made a difference in your life. Take a moment to experience the warm feeling of gratitude that comes from appreciating and thanking this person for the beautiful gifts they have shared with you. We each have a tremendous capacity for making a difference in the lives of others. What one action might you take today to positively affect the quality of another person's life?

I am a generous spirit, giving freely from the abundance in my heart.
I find big-hearted new ways to give to others. I take action
to make a positive difference in the world.

Prayer of Giving

Let generosity of heart and hand begin with me. Help me to create a better world through the giving of my unique gifts, talents and passions. Thank you for all you have given me so I may generously give to others.

Hope

Even if I knew that tomorrow the world would go to pieces, I would still plant my apple tree.

Martin Luther

Hope

I am grateful for Hope.

Hope is filled with promise and faith. When we dare to hope, we dare to believe in a greater reality. Hope is the breathing of positive expectation into the life of our desires. We need the willingness to not only believe in what is possible, but also to challenge what has previously been considered impossible. This desire to stretch the limits and achieve the unimaginable is the seed from which hope springs forth.

All great accomplishments begin as a tiny seed of hope. When that tiny seed is nourished and cared for with positive expectation, encouragement and action, our hopes take root. Therefore, hoping for a brighter day or for a change in a situation is not just wishful thinking. Hope is reduced to wishful thinking only when it is not accompanied by intentional action. We need to remember that prayer is one such intentional action. Hope for your heart's desires and allow well-planned action to bring your desires to fruition.

The teacher, author and peace activist Thich Nhat Hanh said, "Hope is important because it can make the present moment less difficult to bear. If we believe that tomorrow will be better, we can bear a hardship today." No matter what our current set of circumstances or how low we may feel, hope can uplift our spirits, give us strength and faithfully carry us through tough times. Hope encourages us to believe in infinite possibilities and the miracles that lie ahead.

I expect great things to happen. I am filled with hope, faith and optimism. My possibilities are limitless.

Prayer of Hope

Make me a light that radiates your hope into the lives of others.
Breathe into me the joyful expectation of a brighter day.
Thank you for lifting my spirit and giving me
an inner spark of hope.

Imagination

Imagination is the eye of the soul.

Joseph Joubert

Imagination

I am grateful for Imagination.

Imagination is our greatest and most powerful creative tool. Through imagination, we are able to reveal our own soul's infinite potential as well as our ego's worst fears. When we use our imagination for our highest good and for creating our highest vision of ourselves, we are operating from our soul; when we use our imagination for self-sabotage and for creating limitations in our lives, we are functioning from the ego.

The artist Pablo Picasso stated, "Everything you can imagine is real." Creation begins in the imagination. As children, we allowed our imagination to create monsters that lived in the closet and under the bed. The fear we experienced from these imagined villains was very real. Nightmares resulted from these make-believe creations. As adults, we do the same thing, but the bogeyman has morphed into grown-up villains, such as fear of failure, false notions of unworthiness and lack of self-love—all thoughts and ideas we have imagined into being. When we understand and accept that our fears and limitations are only negative expressions of our own imagination, we become inspired to imagine something grand for our lives.

Imagination enthusiastically leads us to discover, create and build things that generate a better world for all of us. Through imagination, we stimulate new possibilities. By becoming aware of the power of our imagination, we can change the course of our destiny. What we can imagine, we can become.

I use my divine imagination to create a new and better reality.
I actively visualize a glorious life that inspires and energizes me.
I now take charge of creatively imagining a magnificent future.

Prayer of Imagination

Guide me in using my imagination to bring into being the life you have intended for me. Help me to clearly imagine and envision that which is in my highest good.
Thank you for the life-enhancing gift of imagination.

Joy

Joy is a net of love by which you can catch souls.

Mother Teresa

Joy
I am grateful for Joy.

Joy is the gleeful expression of the Divine within us. Joy is a state of consciousness—a way of being—while happiness is an emotion or feeling. Happiness comes and goes, but joy remains rooted deeply within our soul. We become aware of the Divine in our lives by appreciating the omnipresent life force in all living beings. When we enjoy the bluebird's cheerful whistle, the soothing trickle of water flowing in a stream, a baby's soft coo or tears of deep gratitude, and recognize something of ourselves in each expression, we experience the Divine and awaken our joy.

The poet Kahlil Gibran wrote, "The deeper that sorrow carves into your being the more joy you can contain." Even if our joy has been suppressed for some time, we needn't worry; it is available to even the most pessimistic or cynical of us. All that is needed is a conscious willingness and heartfelt desire to experience the joy in life. When we release our past regrets and our attempts to control the future, we are free to experience the joy that exists now. Sometimes we need to take a break from our problems and experience a joyful moment in order to bring our life into proper perspective. We are then blessed with a fresh, new outlook on our lives—one that is rich with hope, joy and wonder.

Tapping into the bountiful joy of each day can refresh us and give us the vital energy needed to confront whatever life sends our way. When we walk through our day with joyful anticipation, we invite the magical moments of the day to be revealed to us. Joy is contagious and spreads like dust in the wind. As our awareness shifts into a state of joy, we are able to uplift the consciousness of all those around us. The more we intentionally focus on the pleasant things in life, the more joy we will experience. When we feel joy, we need to immediately acknowledge it with an expression of gratitude. Joy is a tremendous gift.

I am a joyful expression of the Divine. My heart beats with the joyous
rhythm of life. I sprinkle joy and delight into our world.

Prayer of Joy

Help me cultivate and appreciate the joy that exists within
me and all around me. Inspire me to live in joyful celebration.
Thank you for sharing your divine love and infinite joy.

Kindness

Kindness is the golden chain by which society is bound together.

Johann Wolfgang von Goethe

Kindness

I am grateful for Kindness.

Kindness originates from a deep inner well of love and compassion that joins us to the hearts and souls of others. When we are the recipients of a gracious act of kindness, we are appreciative and thankful. When we are the giver of kindness, we usually feel equally as fulfilled as the recipient. A helping hand, a smile, an encouraging word—kindness is expressed through small and generous acts of goodwill. When we live with kindness in our hearts, we continuously send tokens of love into the world. Thoughtful, kindhearted actions can dramatically change the course of our lives without our ever knowing it.

Kindness is inherent in our nature. Just as a baby innately yearns to be held and to hold on, so do we instinctively yearn to receive kindness and give it back in return. Plato taught that we should be kind to everyone, for we all are fighting a battle of some sort. As we reach out to those who are in pain, those who are in need, those who are angry or those who seem to not have any kindness at all to share in return, we help to replenish their well of kindness.

Every demonstration of kindness, large and small, has a ripple effect that expands far beyond the initial act. Indiscriminate acts of loving-kindness erase our sense of separation from one another, bring us into a state of belonging and change our world. Kindness is the invisible chain that links us together in love.

I am overflowing with loving-kindness. I give kindness freely and receive the universal flow of kindness in return. I generously demonstrate compassion and kindness in my daily life.

Prayer of Kindness

Please help me to be a vessel of kindness, positively affecting all with whom I come in contact. Help me to be kind in all the ways I know, as well as the ways with which I am not yet familiar. Thank you for awakening the loving-kindness that you have placed within my soul.

Laughter

At the height of laughter
the universe is flung into a
kaleidoscope of new possibilities.

Jean Houston

Laughter
I am grateful for Laughter.

Laughter uplifts the soul and can bring a lighter perspective to almost any situation. Thankfully, we are born with the capacity to laugh and smile; it is part of our universal human experience. When we are able to laugh, it means our ability to find pleasure in a person or situation has not been lost.

Laughter releases healing endorphins into our bodies that boost our mood and our immune system. It also impacts our pain receptors, making us less sensitive and more resistant to pain. Laughter shakes us out of the seriousness of life. Laughing is not a shirking off of the importance of an issue, but rather a decision not to ignore the amusement buried within the seriousness of a challenge. When we are able to laugh at both our silly and serious predicaments, and even at ourselves, we realize that we have the power to influence how we experience life. Sometimes it is in the most tragic of circumstances that a dose of comic relief and lightheartedness is most needed.

Charlie Chaplin said, "A day without laughter is a day wasted." When we laugh, we choose to explore the world of optimistic possibilities. Laughter is a willingness to see that there are far more than two sides to every coin. When we share lively, playful humor or a deep, roaring belly laugh with a friend, our burdens are lessened and our joys doubled.

I am filled with joyful giggles and irrepressible laughter.
Deep belly laughs frequently and easily bubble up from within me.
I find fun, humor and comic relief in each day.

Prayer of Laughter

Help me to embrace the lighthearted, fun side of life. Embolden me with the ability to spread good-natured, cheerful humor. Thank you for helping me uplift others through your contagious gift of laughter.

Music

Music heals the heart and makes it whole, flows from heaven to the soul.

Unknown

Music

I am grateful for Music.

Music is the rhythmic breath of the Divine moving all around us. Music is in the sound of the leaves rustling in the wind and in the water lapping against the shore. Music can be the familiarity of a loved one's voice, a child's laugh or a Beethoven symphony. Through music, we find the sound of life and the vibration of the universe resonating through us.

Sounds that come together in an arranged and composed manner have the ability to move us passionately and emotionally. When music is created and performed with the intent of promoting beauty and harmony, we feel more closely connected to God, our culture and one another. Whether it is the sounds in nature or the sounds of an instrument, music moves us through varying states of emotional awareness. Music serves as a vehicle for expressing and releasing emotions; it can soothe, inspire, energize and even sadden us.

The Austrian composer and conductor Gustav Mahler said, "If a composer could say what he had to say in words, he would not bother trying to say it in music." Music communicates beyond words because the vibrations and melody speak to us at a higher level of receptivity than language is able to access. Music stirs our soul and alters our consciousness. Take time each day to listen to the music of life, appreciating the many harmonious expressions that surround us.

I attune myself to the melodious and rhythmic sounds in my day.
I listen to inspirational music that feeds my soul and uplifts my spirit.
I rejoice in the beautiful music of life.

Prayer of Music

Guide me in choosing music that resonates with the needs
of my soul. Help me to relish the delightful melodies
that fill our world. Thank you for blessing me with
the precious pleasure of music.

Now

There was never a time when your life was not now, nor will there ever be.

Eckhart Tolle

Now

I am grateful for Now.

Now is the essence of life in the midst of the moment. Being attentive to the now is how we begin to appreciate the aliveness, vitality and wonder within us and all around us. We all hold the capacity to be fully present in the beauty and wonder of the moment. But if we get unduly invested in what lies ahead, it costs us the joy of the now. We may believe that some future event or thing will make our life better, more satisfying or pleasurable than it currently is. This seductive illusion takes our focus away from completely enjoying our day.

Living in the present and planning for the future is a delicate balance. Most of us confuse actively planning for the future with anxiously worrying about the future; however, worry is an ineffective planning tool. A wise person once said, "Worry is like a rocking chair; it gives you something to do, but it doesn't get you anywhere." We may falsely believe that if we spend time obsessively thinking about negative "what-ifs," we will be better prepared for what is to come. The truth is, even if there is a potential crisis on the horizon, we will be better able to deal with it if we cultivate a serene, undisturbed and clear mind from which to stay grounded. From this place of centered strength, we make sounder decisions and take constructive action more easily and readily.

Being entirely present in each moment involves giving our undivided attention, appreciation and love to our current experience. When we are fully present, we are able to enjoy the richness of the now. Our senses become more alive as we become acutely aware of our surroundings. We hear sounds we previously were not conscious of, and we notice the awe-inspiring small details of life. Honoring the sacredness of the now brings us closer to our Creator as we become reverent to all living things that are a part of our present.

I live fully in the now. I embrace the sacredness of each
and every precious moment. I now choose to be keenly
aware of and fascinated by life.

Prayer of Now

Awaken my ability to be completely present in each moment.
Remove any illusions that prevent me from being where my
feet are planted right now. Thank you for your divine presence
in every moment of my life.

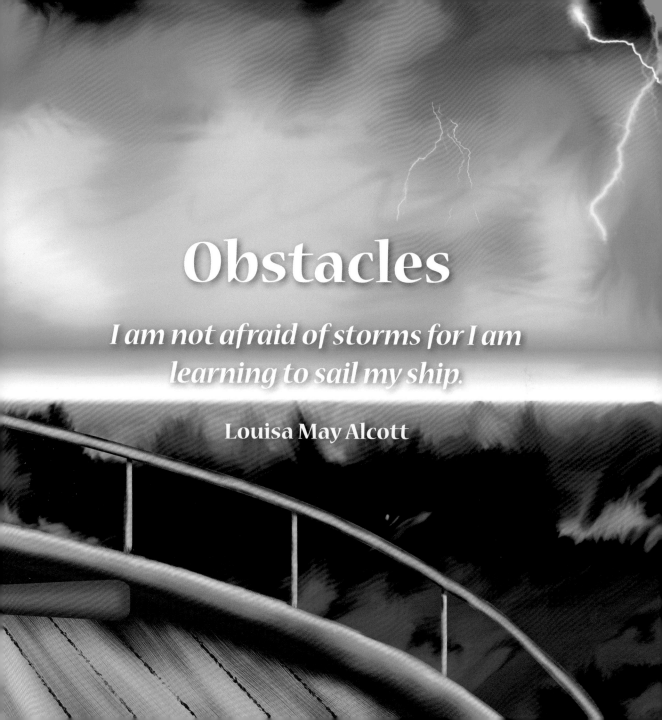

Obstacles

I am not afraid of storms for I am learning to sail my ship.

Louisa May Alcott

Obstacles

I am grateful for Obstacles.

Obstacles are an unavoidable part of our human journey. We all encounter obstacles on our path, but how we choose to navigate through them will determine our success in life. When we were children, we loved to compete in the obstacle course. We excitedly embraced the challenge of overcoming the barriers on our way to the finish line. Whether we had to crawl under, jump over or run around the obstacle, we understood that it was part of the race and what gave the competition its thrill. What we did not realize as children was the tremendous lesson this field day activity would bring to the broader scope of our lives.

The German-born physicist Albert Einstein once said, "In the middle of difficulty lies opportunity." Obstacles are gifts, disguised as difficulties, scattered along the path of life. Many of the blocks that seemingly stand in our way are actually learning opportunities waiting to manifest in our lives. When we can learn how to navigate through an obstacle, rather than become defeated by it, we evolve both personally and spiritually.

We cannot solve our problems or overcome our limitations with the same consciousness that created them. Obstacles energize us to stretch beyond our routine way of thinking and encourage us to try on an unfamiliar behavior or skill. During the process, we improve upon our perceived weaknesses and turn them into unanticipated strengths. By expressing gratitude for the obstacles in our lives, we uncover their hidden treasures and the wealth of support available to us. As we move toward, and many times fly past, the finish line, we find that we are wiser, stronger and more capable than we ever thought possible. We can then look back and realize it was never about the finish line; it was always about the lessons we learned navigating the course.

I embrace the obstacles in my life with courage, integrity and strength.
I choose to see obstacles as opportunities to grow into the best person I can be.
I tap into the infinite wisdom of the universe to reveal optimal solutions.

Prayer of Obstacles

Support me as I confront my fears and move through the obstacles you have lovingly put on my path. Help me to face these life lessons with courage, curiosity and unwavering faith. Thank you for providing me with obstacles that bring me closer to you.

Passion

*From the intricate flower blossoms
the fruit of passion.*

Tatiana Michaels

I am grateful for Passion.

Passion is the life force propelling the purpose-driven life. Our souls' purpose is to have experiences that flame our deepest passions and help us grow into our fullest potential. Only through discovering and realizing our passions do we become confident about the direction for our lives and have the opportunity to find lasting happiness.

Fulfilling our passions is not a selfish act. Quite the contrary, expanding upon our passions is a service we provide to others. The music of Mozart has been the inspiration for untold acts of greatness. Individually, we have been moved by his music, and great artistic work has been created from the monumental force of his passion. Children have been lulled to sleep for generations by his piano version of the tune "Twinkle, Twinkle, Little Star." Dances have been performed and ceremonies conducted all through a love of his profound compositions. By fulfilling his passions, Mozart gave a gift to the world that continues to give unceasingly.

Engaging our passions allows us to be a channel for the Divine. Spiritualist Marianne Williamson says, "We are born to make manifest the glory of God that is within us. It's not just in some of us; it's in everyone. And as we let our own light shine, we unconsciously give other people permission to do the same." When we allow our soul to open up and fulfill its destiny, we pave the road for others to do the same, influencing them in extraordinary ways. Our lives are intended to be passion in action. In order to live fully and completely without regret, we must unleash the passion that vibrantly lives within.

I am filled with unbridled passion and certainty of purpose.
I enthusiastically take steps to fulfill my soul's callings.
I live with exuberance and zest for life!

Prayer of Passion

Reveal to me my passions so that I may live with divine inspiration and authentic purpose. Encourage and support me as I discover, engage and fully enjoy my passions. Thank you for blessing me with an unlimited enthusiasm for life.

Quiet

Only in quiet waters do things mirror themselves undistorted, only in a quiet mind is adequate perception of the world.

Hans Margolius

I am grateful for Quiet.

Quietness heightens and transforms our perception of our experiences. Only through quiet self-reflection are we able to accurately perceive ourselves and gain clarity about the world around us. We all want to live passionate and purposeful lives, but we may mistakenly begin this search in the busyness of the outer world. The first steps in the journey for passion, purpose and ultimately peace of mind begin by looking inside. When we take time to silently journey inward, we cultivate an inner stillness that brings the peace-filled contentment we have been looking for in our fleeting outer activities.

If we are to consistently live with a feeling of genuine fulfillment, we need to foster an inner tranquility that is not dependent upon external life events. Only when we are truly aware of our internal experiences can we grow closer in our cherished relationship with God.

Humanitarian Mother Teresa once said, "See how nature—trees, flowers, grass—grows in silence; see the stars, the moon and the sun, how they move in silence ... we need silence to be able to touch souls." And this includes our own soul. As we dedicate time to wholeheartedly listen to ourselves, we feel intimately connected to the awe of the world within us and around us. We sense the deep serenity that is possible when we travel to our own inner refuge. As we dive into this place of quiet, magical communion, we are no longer swept away by the endless distractions and frantic demands of our turbulent world. The enveloping quietness gently soothes the stirrings of our soul. We realize that all we long for has been found in the wisdom of this quiet moment.

I savor the quiet moments in my day. I lovingly bring attention to my sacred inner life. I choose to devote time to silently be with myself and God.

Prayer of Quiet

Teach me how to be still and quiet so that I may be restored to wholeness. Breathe into me an inner tranquility that I can carry with me throughout my day. Thank you for calming my mind and bringing quiet comfort into my life.

Relationships

If words are the lyrics and laughter the melody, then a relationship becomes a symphony.

Nicholas Sparks

Relationships

I am grateful for Relationships.

Relationships are a symbol of our sacred union with one another and God. We all deeply desire intimate relationships, both platonic and romantic, in which to share the dance of life. We yearn for the companionship and the sense of belonging that come from knowing that we are not alone. But the truth is, we never really are alone. The relationship we share with God is omnipresent, providing us with the solid foundation necessary for all other relationships to grow and flourish.

Before we can have a substantial and rewarding connection with another person, we need to also invest in developing a deeply trusting relationship with ourselves. Astrologer and writer Alice DeVille said, "Each relationship you have with another reflects the relationship you have with yourself." The degree to which we love and respect ourselves will be mirrored in the relationships we draw into our lives. Whatever it is we expect in another, we must first satisfy within ourselves. We must learn to enjoy our own company, be at peace with our own imperfections and give ourselves the love for which we yearn.

Each of our relationships is rich with spiritual opportunities. When we choose to intentionally grow from our relationship experiences, we are better able to integrate these newfound lessons into our lives, becoming wiser and stronger than before. As we grow into our highest vision of ourselves, we attract relationships that express our ever-evolving nature and the longings of our soul.

I deeply and completely love, honor and cherish myself. I am blessed with inspiring, harmonious and fun relationships. I now choose to experience loving relationships that uplift and nourish me.

Prayer of Relationships

Remind me of your faithful presence in all of my relationships. Help me to depend on my connection with you to sustain and comfort me. Thank you for the kind, supportive and encouraging people you have brought into my life.

Serendipity

Serendipity is God's way of remaining anonymous.

Unknown

Serendipity
I am grateful for Serendipity.

Serendipity is the divine timing of the universe. Serendipity occurs when we unexpectedly discover something fortunate while looking for something else entirely. Tobi Tobias, author of the children's book *Serendipity,* writes, "Serendipity is putting a quarter in the gumball machine and having three pieces come rattling out instead of one—all red." This quote captures the delightful nature of serendipity, which some call "luck" or "coincidence." When we appreciate the serendipity present in our lives, we are able to view fortunate coincidences as small miracles. Finding these chance opportunities is what makes life magical and continually surprising.

In the midst of following our dreams, the universe opens and closes many doors in the most unexpected and serendipitous ways. By not resisting the doors that are opening and shutting before us, we allow ourselves to move through life in God's perfect timing. We serendipitously stumble upon people, opportunities and situations that positively influence our lives. By not forcing through doors that appear closed, but rather faithfully walking with joyous anticipation through the doors that are open, we arrive, one step at a time, at wondrous life destinations.

In order to recognize the serendipity in our lives, we need to take positive actions to reach our goals while remaining detached from specific outcomes. This means that we confidently pursue our dreams without worrying about the precise details of how they will be fulfilled. When we trust our intuition and faithfully follow our hearts' desires, serendipity frequently occurs in our lives. We develop a keen awareness of how God's miracles are unfolding for us in the most magical ways. More often than not, we gloriously arrive at a destination that is far beyond our wildest imagination.

I have confidence in the serendipity of the universe. I release my
preconceived notions and trust the perfection of divine timing.
I see the unexpected and delightful surprises that fill my day.

Prayer of Serendipity

Align my life with your divine timing. Heighten my awareness of the serendipitous miracles that you have sprinkled along my path. Thank you for gracing my life with the magic of serendipity.

Touch

*To touch someone is to share the
spark that is life.*

Hansi Nurit Pilzer

Touch

I am grateful for Touch.

Touch is one of the most effective ways to communicate love. In our technology-enhanced world, many of us have lost the essential element of human touch that once united us. Similar to the immediate access we have to one another through the Internet, touch instantly connects us to each other's hearts and souls. Physical contact elevates our interactions to a level beyond the spoken or written word, providing us with much-needed nonverbal reassurance, support and affection. The comfort of a hug and the warmth of a held hand bring to life the healing spark of touch.

Whether we are young or old, rich or poor, sick or healthy, we all welcome touch that is loving and respectful. We feel comforted, more alive and satisfied when we share the close bond that emerges from physical tenderness. Diana, Princess of Wales, said, "Yes, I do touch. I believe that everyone needs that." Princess Diana innately understood the power of touch and the remarkable therapeutic effects that it holds. The degree to which we are able to reach out and touch others is a sign of our humanity.

Touch has great healing power and is vital for our physical, spiritual and emotional well-being. It offers us immediate stress relief and a shelter from the worries of the day. Research suggests that regular touch boosts our immune system and can actually add years to our lives. Whether it is through hugging a friend, a lover, a sister, a mother or even a stranger in need, touch provides us with a sense of solace, security and intimacy. When we touch someone, we are touched in return.

*I welcome loving touch into my life. I generously and respectfully
share the precious gift of touch. I stretch beyond my comfort zone to
affectionately touch another.*

Prayer of Touch

Show me how to graciously give and receive loving touch.
Help me to use your gift of touch to heal, encourage and strengthen.
Thank you for the restorative power of touch.

Understanding

The noblest pleasure is the joy of understanding.

Leonardo da Vinci

Understanding

I am grateful for Understanding.

Understanding allows us to experience compassion and kindness toward each other. More than just the receiving and processing of knowledge, understanding involves empathetically and accurately perceiving another person's situation and the needs prompting their actions or words. We all want our needs and desires to be heard and the reasons we behave or act the way we do to be understood. When we intentionally unhook from our personal objectives to truly understand another's point of view, we begin the process of living together in peace.

We all have had different life experiences and influences that have molded our personalities, opinions and behaviors. We may feel frustrated or become critical when someone else's actions, feelings or thoughts contrast with our own. Swiss psychoanalyst Carl G. Jung said, "Everything that irritates us about others can lead us to an understanding of ourselves." Sometimes what bothers us most about someone else is what we unconsciously do not accept about ourselves. Therefore, the more we can understand and accept ourselves, the more tolerance we develop toward others. Self-awareness is vital in having empathy for other people's feelings, perspectives and actions.

An essential component of understanding is compassionate, nonjudgmental and attentive listening. Lack of empathetic listening is one of the primary causes of interpersonal difficulties and relationship dissatisfaction. By patiently listening in a kindhearted, curious and tolerant manner, we can cultivate the type of loving understanding we wish to receive.

I am an open-minded, compassionate and understanding person.
I celebrate diversity by giving others the same respect, understanding
and appreciation that I want for myself. I am an agent of tolerance
and peace in the world.

Prayer of Understanding

Utilize me as a conduit for your understanding, love and grace. Help me to humbly release my need to be right as I strive to better understand others. Thank you for illuminating my heart with the light of understanding.

Voice

In voicing our truth, we find the depth of our power.

Michele Wahlder

I am grateful for Voice.

Voicing our souls' inner truth is an act of empowerment. Many of us were taught as children to be nice, stay quiet and just listen. While these are important qualities, if we completely abandon our truth to keep relational harmony, we are essentially being unfaithful and disloyal to ourselves. Chinese thinker and social philosopher Confucius teaches that our words are the voice of the heart. When we silence our voice, we silence the message of our heart. Our soul longs to be expressed through our voice. In order to live authentically and vibrantly, we must honor our voice by verbalizing our thoughts and feelings. Confidently communicating our inner truth liberates and enlivens our spirit.

All too often we silence our voice out of fear of rejection or criticism. We may mistakenly believe that someone else knows better than us. Perhaps they do, but without respectfully voicing our opinion, we will never have a genuine opportunity to understand and learn from one another. When we speak out courageously, honestly and boldly, we move our inner voice out of our bodies, releasing a powerful energy of thought into the world. Albert Einstein wisely said, "Nothing that I can do will change the structure of the universe. But maybe, by raising my voice, I can help the greatest of all causes—goodwill among men and peace on Earth."

Our voice is the protective and loving presence that establishes our personal boundaries and provides instructions to others on how we prefer to be treated. Voicing our desires, preferences and opinions allows us to define ourselves and what we want for our lives. When we bravely express ourselves, we experience an inner power that inspires, energizes and strengthens us. Speak out and honor your voice.

I use my voice to authentically communicate my soul's inner wisdom and truth. I honor myself by clearly voicing my needs and preferences. I allow my voice to be a guardian of my heart and a cheerleader for my desires.

Prayer of Voice

Make my voice a loving instrument that I can depend on to communicate your all-knowing wisdom and truth. Give me the confidence to courageously express myself for the highest good of all. Thank you for empowering me with a strong, clear voice that will not be silenced.

Work

Work and play are words used to describe the same thing under different circumstances.

Mark Twain

I am grateful for Work.

Work is ideally an adult version of play. When we are blessed to find work that feels like play, we are naturally motivated and inspired. We feel the joy that comes from being able to fully express our natural talents while serving humanity. When we can enthusiastically say that we love our work, we know it has truly become our passion. Arriving at this place of "work joy" is a dynamic journey that requires time and patience.

In the progression toward our "life's work," we need to take time to appreciate every stage of the journey. As we travel along our work path, we have frequent opportunities to make contributions to the greater good. Being conscious of these opportunities helps us to transform what we may perceive to be even the most menial tasks into a gracious chance to serve. Imagine the most modest of jobs: perhaps it is the janitor at the office, the housekeeper or the garbage collector. Now imagine life without this person's contribution. We each make a tremendous impact on the world, no matter how seemingly small or inconsequential our job.

We all aspire to greatness and need to remain dedicated to experiencing work that most fully utilizes our unique strengths and passions. None of us wants to settle for work that is less than what we ultimately desire; however, at times we may need to take temporary transition jobs. These bridge jobs can be easier to accept and appreciate when we understand that they too provide us with opportunities to positively serve our society and grow as people. Author and political activist Helen Keller said, "The world is moved along, not only by the mighty shoves of its heroes, but also by the aggregate of the tiny pushes of each honest worker." When we consciously intend to make a sincere contribution wherever we are on our career path, we awaken our greatness within.

I accomplish humble work tasks as though they were great and noble.
I joyfully express my passions, gifts and strengths through my life's work.
I am proud of how my work positively contributes to society.

Prayer of Work

Bless me with work that enlivens my spirit and contributes to the greater good. Help me to experience work as a playful expression of my natural passions and talents. Thank you for guiding me along the path of my life's work.

eX's

*The past should be a springboard,
not a hammock.*

Ivern Ball

I am grateful for eX's.

X relationships can be stepping-stones to a higher vision of ourselves. Some people come into our lives for a lifetime, while others impact our lives in a relatively brief period of time. We should never consider any past relationships—marriages, friendships or family relationships—as failures, but rather as precious, hard-earned lessons to be cherished, respected and held in a place of deep gratitude. These previous relationships serve to strengthen and mold our character.

We unconsciously attract people into our lives at certain times to reciprocally provide lessons that will allow our souls to evolve. As we flow into and out of relationships, we have a choice of whether to learn and grow or harbor resentment and anger from our experiences. Sometimes it takes years to get clarity regarding why particular relationships were brought into our lives, especially painful ones. We can have faith, even if we cannot fully comprehend the reasons, that in the divine scheme of things, there was always a higher intelligence at work, guiding us as we spiritually evolved.

When we "get" the lesson, we cease attracting that particular type of relationship. We then move into new relationships that continue to challenge and expand our capacity to give and receive love. Time was never wasted in our ex-relationships, as they assisted us in transforming into more positive, enlightened and authentic versions of ourselves.

I appreciate and cherish the memories, lessons and gifts of my past. I now free myself of all resentment and anger. I lovingly forgive and release my past relationships and boldly move forward with my life.

Prayer of eX's

Help me to be grateful for all my ex-relationships. Guide me as I learn from the valuable lessons each person has brought into my life. Thank you for bringing perfect relationships into my life for my optimal spiritual growth.

Yes

The universal answer is always yes.

Gabrielle Fontane

Yes

I am grateful for Yes.

Yes is the most affirmative response we can have to life. When Moses asked the burning bush what or who it was, the response he received was *"Ehyeh asher ehyeh"* (Exodus 3:14). Translated in English, this means "I am that I am." One interpretation of what God was telling Moses is that we all become whatever it is we proclaim for ourselves: I am whatever it is that I proclaim that I am. Louise Hay, spiritual teacher and author, said, "Every thought we think is creating our future." As we think, so shall we become.

The universal answer to every "I am" statement or thought is always a resounding "yes." The current reality of each moment is the affirmative answer to a previous "I am" statement. So, when we say to ourselves, *I am so stupid,* the universe responds with "yes." *I am sick. I am fat. I am broke. I could never do that.* Yes. Yes. Yes.

The power of "yes" is life transforming. When we replace our negative belief statements with positive ones, the answer remains the same—yes. *I am filled with divine energy. I am financially abundant. I always have more than enough. I am beautiful. I am loved. I am perfect, whole and complete.* The universal reply is still the same—yes. When we make positive changes to our outdated thought patterns and affirm these changes in word and deed, we raise our consciousness and the energy that surrounds us. As our energetic vibration elevates, we begin to transform our lives and the lives of those around us in miraculous ways. We become more powerful, inspiring and beautiful as we claim the power of "yes."

I am happy, healthy and filled with joy.
I am alive with creative energy and vitality.
I say "yes" to life!

Prayer of Yes

Fill me with uplifting, life-enhancing messages that reflect my highest nature. Help me to proclaim "yes" to honoring the magnificence in myself and receiving the best in life. Thank you for the universal "yes" that shapes my life.

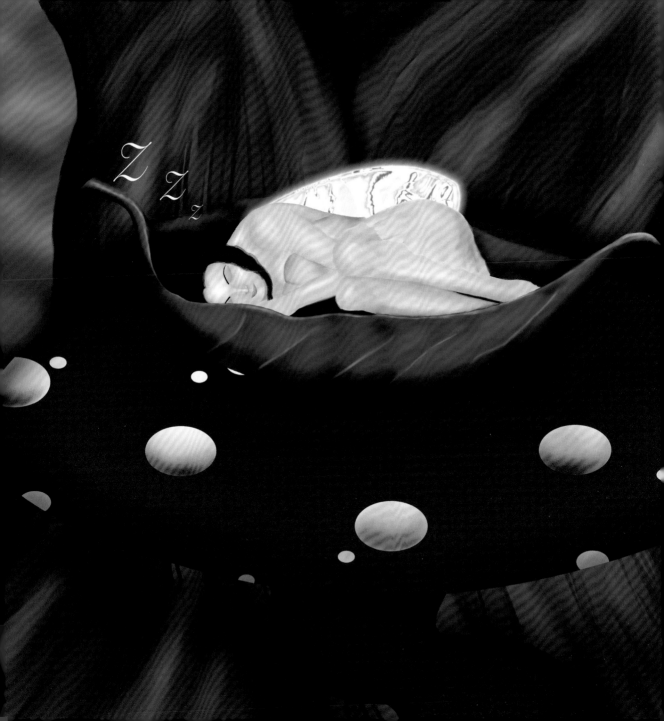

Zzz ... Sleep

*And if tonight my soul may find
her peace in sleep, and sink in good
oblivion, and in the morning
wake like a new-opened flower, then
I have been dipped again in God,
and new-created.*

D. H. Lawrence

I am grateful for Zzz ... Sleep.

Zzz ... Sleep is a time of physical restoration, mental rejuvenation and spiritual renewal. We often exhaust ourselves by packing too many things into our day, making it difficult to unwind when it is time for much-needed rest. When we cut down on our sleep, it makes us more sensitive to the effects of daily stressors, more easily irritated and far less productive. A chronic lack of sleep can decrease our bodies' natural ability to cope, thereby increasing our risk of physical and emotional ills. Quality sleep is absolutely vital if we are to achieve our true potential.

We can influence the quality of our sleep by incorporating rituals that calm the mind and promote relaxation, contributing to a more peaceful night's sleep. Create a ritual of turning the television and computer off early, slipping on cozy pajamas, dimming bright lights, soaking in a warm, fragrant bath and reading a comforting book or any other calming habit. The simple structure of the alphabet can be used as a practical tool to help you reflect upon people, places and things that you are grateful for as you drift off to sleep. Journaling or mentally reviewing what is good and right in your world at bedtime will create a positive mind-set from which sleep can gently wash over you.

While we sleep, our subconscious is able to communicate to us without interference from our ego. In this place of nonresistance, God provides healing for our bodies, minds and souls. When we invite God and the angels into our sleep time, we miraculously receive messages that reveal answers to our most perplexing questions and solutions to our most troubling problems. British poet Lord Byron said, "Sleep hath its own world." During sleep, we access more than our logical minds; we connect with the imaginative world of dreams and images. This resourceful world can shed new light on whatever daunting issue we have been dealing with in our waking life.

***I easily relax into peaceful sleep. I sleep soundly and wake
in the morning feeling rested, refreshed and rejuvenated.
I trust the divine process of sleep.***

Prayer of Zzz ... Sleep

Restore and heal me as I sleep. Fill me with the direction and guidance I need for my waking hours. Thank you for your protective presence as I drift into peaceful dreams.

About the Author

Michele Wahlder, MS, LPC, PCC, is an internationally recognized life coach, career counselor, speaker and gratitude enthusiast. She is the founder of Life Possibilities, LLC, a company that champions people to become the highest vision they hold for themselves in their lives, careers and relationships through the vehicles of coaching, seminars and books. Wahlder delights in helping her clients discover their strengths, passions and purpose so that their outer lives authentically reflect their hearts' desires. She has worked with numerous organizations, including Match.com, *Fitness* magazine, Lucent Technologies and Girls, Inc., to improve individual performance and organizational effectiveness.

Wahlder is a popular guest on television and radio, including WFAA-TV's *Good Morning Texas*, KDAF-TV's *The 33 News* and CBS and CNN Radio. She holds a master's degree in Counseling Education from Texas Woman's University, is licensed by the state of Texas as a Licensed Professional Counselor and is certified through the International Coach Federation as a Professional Certified Coach. Honored as the Global Career Spokesperson for Bayer's Global MS Awareness Campaign, Wahlder understands firsthand the challenges associated with surviving a life-threatening illness and has allowed the experience to make her a stronger, more compassionate and grateful person. She continues to volunteer for several nonprofit organizations that offer adults and children opportunities to enhance their lives and pursue their dreams. Wahlder lives in Dallas, TX, with her fiancé Michael, "bonus daughter" Zoe and Portuguese water dog Moses.

Learn more about Michele Wahlder at:

alphatudes.com

lifepossibilities.com

michelewahlder.com

Michele Wahlder is available for individual and group coaching, television and radio interviews, speaking engagements, workshop training and as a contributing editor for feature articles.

Olivia Newton-John
"Grace and Gratitude"
Written by Olivia Newton-John and Amy Sky
OliviaNewton-John.com

Olivia Newton-John has graciously provided a musical gift to enhance your gratitude experience.

Please enjoy a **FREE DOWNLOAD** of her beautifully healing song "Grace and Gratitude" at: **OliviaNewton-John.com/alphatudes**